The Art of
Comics

Other titles in the *Art Scene* series include:

ART SCENE

The Art of
Comics

Stuart A. Kallen

ReferencePoint
Press®

San Diego, CA

© 2020 ReferencePoint Press, Inc.
Printed in the United States

For more information, contact:
ReferencePoint Press, Inc.
PO Box 27779
San Diego, CA 92198
www.ReferencePointPress.com

LIBRARY OF CONGRESS CATALOGING-IN-PUBLICATION DATA

Name: Kallen, Stuart A., 1955– author.
Title: The Art of Comics/by Stuart A. Kallen.
Description: San Diego, CA: ReferencePoint Press, Inc., 2020. | Series: Art
  Scene | Includes bibliographical references and index. | Audience: Grades:
  9–12.
Identifiers: LCCN 2018051793 (print) | LCCN 2018057790 (ebook) | ISBN
  9781682825822 (eBook) | ISBN 9781682825815 (hardback)
Subjects: LCSH: Comic books, strips, etc.—History and criticism—Juvenile
  literature. | Graphic novels—History and criticism—Juvenile literature.
Classification: LCC PN6710 (ebook) | LCC PN6710 .K26 2020 (print) | DDC
  741.5/9—dc23
LC record available at https://lccn.loc.gov/2018051793

Contents

The Changing Culture of Comic Books

Comic books have attracted millions of devoted followers since Superman first appeared on the cover of the first issue of *Action Comics* in 1938. Superman's phenomenal success inspired comic book artists to create other superheroes. Over time Spider-Man, the Hulk, Batman, and many others have become icons of American pop culture. The stories that featured these characters for the most part presented classic battles between good and evil. As comic book enthusiast David Youngquist describes it, "Bad guy shows up. Good guy shows up to counter him. They talk trash, throw down, and one of them wins. . . . Repeat next month."[1]

This simple formula worked for decades, but in recent years many artists and other comic book enthusiasts noticed that something was missing. Aside from Black Panther and Wonder Woman, the comic world of good and evil included almost no strong or valiant women, people of color, or characters who did not quite fit into the mainstream population. Superheroes were mostly white males who conformed to gender stereotypes. As Youngquist writes, "Superheroes didn't have love lives, and everyone was straight as a string."[2]

New and Different Comics

The faces of comic book characters—and the stories in which they were featured—changed during the twenty-first century as artists and writers began experimenting with nontraditional characters and themes. These new characters and story lines have generated their own strong following among longtime comic enthusiasts and newer, younger fans. Steve Orlando, who re-created the character Midnighter as a gay superhero in 2015, describes the appeal of nontraditional comic characters: "People tell me that Midnighter gave them the strength to be who they are. Some had waited their whole life for a character that looks like them. And that's what everyone deserves—a . . . moment where [they] say, Hey, that guy's just like me. And that guy's a hero. Maybe I could be a hero too."[3]

Midnighter is just one of many characters that have brought increased diversity to the comic book world. In 2014 Marvel charted a new course with its All-New, All-Different publishing line meant to broaden its appeal to those often ignored in comic books. Marvel launched thirteen comics in which traditional male superheroes were reimagined as female, Latino, African American, or Asian American characters. The hammer of Thor was wielded by a goddess named Mjolnir. The powers of the Hulk were absorbed by a Korean American teenage genius named Amadeus Cho. Spider-Man appeared as a half black, half Puerto Rican character named Miles Morales. While some comics fans are happy to see characters more like themselves, others have noted that the creators of these new comics are still mostly men (106 men to be precise). Only a handful of female artists (including Helen Chen, Stephanie Hans, Stacey Lee, and Sara Pichelli) were working on character reboots at Marvel.

Beyond the Mask

Beyond the big publishers, a new generation of artists and writers is at work reimagining traditional comic themes. They are demanding—and finding—their voices in this long-popular genre. The artists are creating new and different story lines populated by a diverse array of characters. And many are finding new readers through webcomics and graphic novels. These outlets have helped independent artists reach people who have not traditionally been fans of comics. This, in turn, has given new life to comics and those who make them. As *Gotham Academy* artist Becky Cloonan explains, "Being more inclusive allows for more diverse stories to be

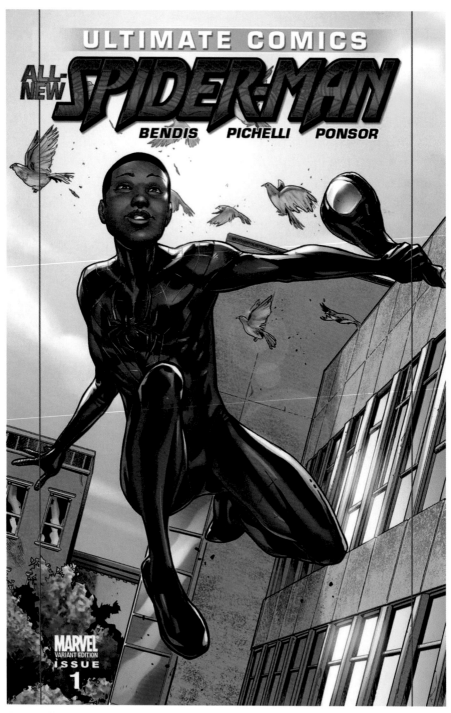

Marvel Comics has begun featuring a new Spider-Man, Miles Morales, who is half African American and half Puerto Rican.

told, which in turn allows for a larger readership, which feeds back into allowing for more creators."[4]

The stories being told by independent artists are often far different from those found on the pages of conventional comic books. Two graphic novels published in 2016 exemplify this trend. *Ghosts* by Raina Telgmeier is about a girl coming to terms with her little sister's serious illness. *Robot Dreams* by Sara Varon tells a bittersweet story about a robot and a dog entirely in pictures. When the robot rusts, the dog tries to fill the emotional void left by the loss with a series of relationships, including one with a melting snowman. Other independent comic artists have reached new audiences through stories about their own lives and their struggles with racism, sexism, and homophobia.

> "Being more inclusive allows for more diverse stories to be told, which in turn allows for a larger readership."[4]
>
> —Comic artist Becky Cloonan

Reimagining the Future

The comic book industry has benefited from the changing demographics of its readers. In 2018 sales of comic books and graphic novels amounted to more than $1 billion. According to Diamond Comic Distributors, the two biggest publishers, DC Comics and Marvel, accounted for most (about 70 percent) of those sales. Independent publishers sold less (about 20 percent). Less than 10 percent of sales (about $90 million) went to artists and writers who sell their work on their personal websites or self-publish on digital platforms like Comixology.

While independent comic book artists might struggle to pay their bills, they have the freedom to make strong political statements through their art. They can also flourish in an industry that is changing rapidly. As comics publisher Regine L. Sawyer says to comic book artists of color, "Creativity can take you anywhere including getting a job, and living, and thriving. Whatever your dreams you can make it happen with hard work and determination."[5]

Sawyer's words ring true for any artist hoping to break into an industry built on superpowers, supervillains, and other make-believe. Since comic books first appeared on newsstands during the Great Depression, they have reflected nearly every aspect of American culture. Whatever the fears, hopes, and dreams of people in a changing world, comic book artists will be there to illustrate the good and the bad, using panels on a page to reimagine the future as the inclusive and diverse world they wish it to be.

CHAPTER ONE

A Brief History of Comic Art

During the nineties, a comic character took America by storm and set off a marketing bonanza. The character was used to sell chewing gum, dolls, clothes, and even whiskey. But it was not Deadpool, Hellboy, nor one of the X-Men, and the decade was not the 1990s. The year was 1895, and the comic character beloved by millions was Yellow Kid, featured in the comic strip *Hogan's Alley*. Yellow Kid was a bald, bucktoothed orphan who wore a yellow oversized nightshirt printed with cartoon punch lines. He was the creation of artist R.F. Outcault, who surrounded Yellow Kid with a mischievous group of children living in New York City's extensive slums. The wry observations of the characters mocked the class and racial tensions that marked city life at that time.

The success of Yellow Kid set off a comic strip boom in the United States. Sunday newspapers introduced a section called the funny pages, filled with comic strips that used four or five panels in a sequence. The comics were printed in full color, which prompted the publisher William Randolph Hearst to exclaim that the funny pages of his *New York Journal* featured "eight pages of iridescent polychromous effulgence that makes the rainbow look like a piece of lead pipe!"[6] It is unclear how many of Hearst's readers understood that "iridescent polychromous effulgence" meant shimmering, multicolored brightness. But by the 1920s, characters from the Sunday funnies like Little Orphan Annie, Felix the Cat, and Popeye the Sailor were as famous as real-life movie stars and sports heroes. As the renowned Japanese cartoonist

Ippei Okamoto noted after visiting New York City in 1923, "American comics have become an entertainment equal to baseball, motion pictures, and the presidential elections."[7]

A Golden Age

By the late 1920s many of the most popular comic strips in the funny pages were based on tales from magazines made from cheap wood pulp paper. Known as pulp-fiction heroes, characters such as Buck Rogers and John Carter of Mars were featured in science fiction stories and popular comics. Crime fighters like the masked Zorro and the mysterious Shadow fought evil villains. Tarzan of the jungle was a daring adventurer.

"The arrival of Superman . . . signaled the moment when the comic book industry came into its own . . . with stories that directly appealed to a younger, male audience."[8]

—Robert Petersen, comic book historian

Tarzan, Buck Rogers, and other pulp-fiction heroes provided inspiration to a Cleveland comic artist named Joe Shuster. In 1933 nineteen-year-old Shuster created Superman. The character had the perfect physique of Tarzan, the ability to leap great distances like John Carter, and the hatred of criminals displayed by the Shadow. Like Zorro's *Z*, the *S* on Superman's chest identified the character with a single letter.

Shuster worked with writer Jerry Siegel, his high school friend, to create numerous Superman comic strips. But no one would publish the work. The idea of a superhuman who could fly at the speed of light, lift ocean liners, and see through objects using X-ray vision was considered too preposterous even by pulp-fiction standards. Superman would not appear in print until 1938, when publisher Max Gaines featured the Man of Steel in the first issue of a new comic book, *Action Comics*.

Although publishers might not have seen the appeal of a character like Superman, fans clamored for more. Crowds of mostly ten- to twelve-year-old boys began demanding the latest *Action*

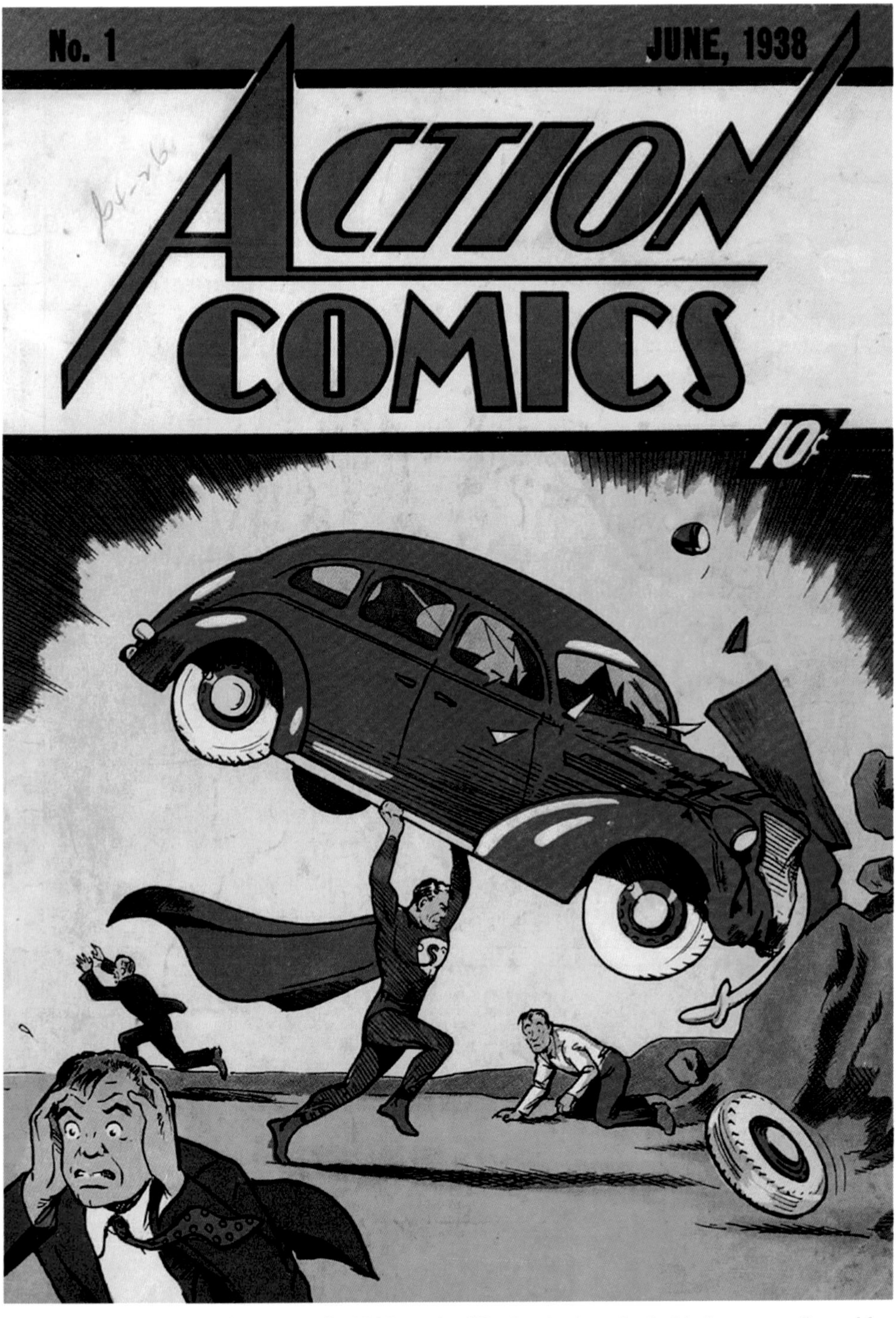
No. 1
JUNE, 1938
ACTION COMICS
10¢

The first appearance of Superman in 1938 marked the beginning of what is known as the golden age of comics.

The First Comic Books

During the 1930s, young readers made the funny pages the most popular part of every newspaper. As comic book historians Fred Van Lente and Ryan Dunlavey explain, "For over three decades American children had been throwing out every other section of the newspaper to get their hands on the funnies." Max Gaines, a salesperson at a Connecticut printing company, thought it would be a good idea to eliminate the rest of the newspaper and offer kids what they really wanted: a booklet filled with full-color Sunday funnies comic strips. In 1933 Gaines published the thirty-six-page *Famous Funnies: A Carnival of Comics*—and the American comic book was born.

The success of Gaines's single-issue comic book inspired him to do a series. Working with Dell Publishing, in 1934 he produced the sixty-eight-page *Famous Funnies*. The comic book sold for ten cents and was filled with popular characters of the era, including Good Deed Dotty, High-Gear Homer, Hairsbreadth Harry, Simp O'Dill, and Donald Dare the Demon Reporter. Gaines printed 180,000 copies of this first issue of *Famous Funnies*, and they were quickly snapped up by readers. Other publishers rushed to imitate the successful venture. Dell published 218 monthly issues of *Famous Funnies*, until the title was retired in 1955.

Fred Van Lente and Ryan Dunlavey, *The Comic Book History of Comics*. San Diego: IDW, 2012, p. 26.

Comics at their local newsstands. Comic book historian Robert Petersen explains the phenomenon:

> The arrival of Superman . . . signaled the moment when the comic book industry came into its own and embraced the advantages of a longer format with stories that directly appealed to a younger, male audience. . . . It became increasingly obvious that large numbers of youths were buying Superman comics and that the popularity of this strangely costumed character was spilling over into other comic book titles.[8]

The publishing company that would become DC Comics created the first Superman imitator. In 1939 writer Bob Kane and artist Bill Finger created *The Bat-Man* (later changed to *Batman*). The entire idea for the comic came from Finger's drawing of a costume. The artist gave Batman a wing-like cape, a pointy-eared hood, and eyes that were pure white. While the flat backgrounds and oddly contorted faces drawn by Finger were primitive, Batman was an instant hit.

Other superheroes quickly followed during a period referred to as the golden age of comics. Comic book historians Fred Van Lente and Ryan Dunlavey describe the growing interest in comics: "Starting in 1940 the Superman imitators proliferated faster than a speeding bullet. Every struggling . . . publisher and [comic] strip artist wannabe attempted to strike it rich copying Siegel and Shuster's success."[9] At least 150 new comic book titles appeared, and DC Comics alone created dozens of characters, including Captain America, Green Lantern, the Flash, and Aquaman.

Not all superheroes were men in tights. In 1941 the husband-and-wife team of William Moulton Marston and Elizabeth Marston created Wonder Woman. The Marstons were research psychologists who believed girls also needed a superhero role model. And with her red, white, and blue costume emblazoned with a golden eagle on the chest, Wonder Woman provided an alternative to male characters who conquered and killed their enemies. As William Moulton Marston wrote in 1943, "Wonder Woman saves her worst enemies and reforms their characters. If the incredible barrage of comic strips now assaulting American minds establishes this new definition of heroics in the thought reflexes of the rising generation, it will have been worth many times its weight in pulp paper and multicolored ink."[10]

Great Art and Cinematic Style

The Marstons might have been trying to reshape young American minds, but most comic book creators of the golden age did not attempt to achieve such noble goals. The tales they told were easy to understand, and the artwork was basic. Artists did not use shading or perspective to make scenes seem realistic. Colors were dull, pages were laid out in monotonous square grids, and many panels were filled with dialogue rather than imagery. Comic book artist Will Eisner was unhappy with the crude artwork. He believed that comic books should express the highest artistic standards.

Eisner achieved widespread recognition in 1940 for his Sunday comic strip *The Spirit*, featuring a masked crime fighter by the same name who lived in a hideout under a tombstone in a cemetery. Eisner says *The Spirit* artwork was inspired by early nineteenth-century painter J.M.W. Turner, who was part of the Romantic art movement. Turner's oil paintings of shipwrecks and disasters, which featured spectacular black clouds, lightning, and churning seas, would not be out of place in a modern graphic novel. Eisner also took inspiration from twentieth-century Expressionist painters who used shadows, swirling lines, and distorted perspective to evoke rage, grief, terror, and other emotions.

Even as Eisner found inspiration in the past, he also took artistic cues from cinema, depicting scenes as if they were shots in a movie. Petersen explains that Eisner used "tight framing that cropped figures, dark shadows that enveloped the scenes, and acutely angled compositions at either a bird's eye or worm's eye view."[11] Eisner introduced other innovative filmmaking concepts to comics, including dream sequences, flashbacks, and the foreshadowing of future events. He was also the first to use a splash page, which is an entire page featuring a single dramatic image meant to grab the readers' attention while setting the mood for the story that followed.

Horror and Comic Book Burnings

As the art of comics improved, so did sales. By 1950 about 200 million comic books were published every month. As publishers struggled to produce dozens of titles, they turned to assembly-line techniques that resulted in a division of labor among comic book artists. Those known as pencillers made pencil sketches that provided the main artwork of each comic. The illustrations were colored in by artists called inkers, who used pens or brushes to add shading, depth, and definition to the images.

A Boy Scout leader feeds a bonfire with comic books. Outraged by the grisly images and violent story lines featured in some comic books, a number of civic leaders organized public burnings of such publications.

Increased competition among a growing number of companies fostered a new age of creativity. Artists and writers moved beyond the exploits of superheroes; their stories and drawings began to feature soldiers, cowboys, animals, lovers, and even characters from the Bible. But the best-selling publications were the gruesome horror comics published by Entertaining Comics (EC), a company founded by Bill Gaines, the son of Max Gaines. During the early 1950s, EC published titles like *Vault of Horror*, *Haunt of Fear*, and *Weird Science*. EC's *Tales from the Crypt* featured the sinister Crypt-Keeper, who hosted stories like "The Corpse Nobody Knew," "Zombie!," and "The Hungry Grave." The stories were filled with cruel humor and bizarre, carnival-like characters wielding axes, knives, hypodermic needles, and other implements of torture and death. Kids who were tired of caped crusaders and heroic soldiers snapped up EC comics, which spawned a host of imitators trying to cash in on weird and gory comics.

The work of EC artists, including Al Feldstein, Harvey Kurtzman, and Wally Wood, influenced generations of comic book artists. But during the 1950s some politicians, religious leaders, and others were alarmed by the grisly images and violent story lines found in some of the era's best-selling comic books. This led to a 1954 televised Senate hearing that blamed juvenile delinquency on the proliferation of EC horror comic books. After the hearing, some scout troops and religious groups organized public burnings of comic books to express their outrage at the images being marketed to kids.

Faced with the threat of government censorship, thirty-eight publishers joined together to create the Comics Code Authority (CCA). This organization created the Comics Code to restrict what readers would see in comic books. The Comics Code banned depictions of sex, drugs, and violence and any titles that included the words *crime*, *horror*, and *terror*. The entire EC line used those words, forcing Gaines to shut down the business. (Gaines, Feldstein, and Kurtzman went on to publish *Mad*, an irreverent satire magazine that appealed to millions of baby boomers who were entering their teenage years.) But as Van Lente and Dunlavey write, the CCA changed the face of the comic book business: "The Code's content restrictions . . . [destroyed] comics' ability to appeal to readers who had reached puberty and beyond. Anyone interested in producing more adult material was essentially run out of business."[12] This trend saw the number of published comic book titles drop by more than 50 percent between 1954 and 1956.

The Return of the Superheroes

CCA restrictions led publishers to return to the superhero format. This period, known as the silver age of comics, saw the rise of DC

The Comics Code

In 1954 publishers formed the Comics Code Authority (CCA) to self-regulate the content of comic books. Comic book covers were stamped with the CCA seal of approval to notify parents that the content conformed to the code, which required respect for government, parents, and police. It also banned slang words and bad grammar. Marvel withdrew from the CCA in 2001, leading other comics publishers to ignore the restrictions in the Comics Code. Excerpts from the code are printed below:

- Crimes shall never be presented in such a way as to create sympathy for the criminal, to promote distrust of the forces of law and justice, or to inspire others with a desire to imitate criminals. . . .
- Criminals shall not be presented so as to be rendered glamorous or to occupy a position which creates a desire for emulation.
- In every instance good shall triumph over evil and the criminal punished for his misdeeds.
- Scenes of excessive violence shall be prohibited. Scenes of brutal torture, excessive and unnecessary knife and gunplay, physical agony, gory and gruesome crime shall be eliminated. . . .
- No comic magazine shall use the word horror or terror in its title. . . .
- All lurid, unsavory, gruesome illustrations shall be eliminated. . . .
- [Depictions of the] walking dead, torture, vampires and vampirism, ghouls, cannibalism, and werewolfism are prohibited. . . .
- Females shall be drawn realistically without exaggeration of any physical qualities. . . .
- Respect for parents, the moral code, and for honorable behavior shall be fostered. A sympathetic understanding of the problems of love is not a license for morbid distortion.

Comics Magazine Association of America, "The Comics Code of 1954," Comic Book Legal Defense Fund, 2018. http://cbldf.org.

and Marvel Comics as the dominant forces in the industry. DC was at the forefront of the superhero revival in 1956 when it revamped the Flash, a character first introduced in 1949.

Penciller Carmine Infantino and inker Joe Kubert drew the Flash as a sleek, modernized crime fighter who embodied the optimism and ideals of postwar America. As illustrator and comic book historian Arlen Schumer explains, "The cities the Flash ran through were stylized compositions of futuristically slanted spires. . . . Infantino's trademark long, low panels filled with trim, lithe figures were as sleek and streamlined as the . . . cars of the era. Everything Infantino drew reflected the crystal-clean images of America [promoted] by Hollywood."[13]

Readers snapped up Flash comics as fast as they could be printed. In 2001 Infantino explained how the reintroduction of the character changed everything: "The Flash jump-started the whole superhero business again, and went a long way in saving the comic book business from extinction. DC followed with Green Lantern and then a whole group of superheroes. So the Flash started the superhero party all over again."[14]

> "The Flash . . . went a long way in saving the comic book business from extinction. DC followed with Green Lantern and then a whole group of super-heroes. So the Flash started the superhero party all over again."[14]
>
> —Carmine Infantino, comic book artist

The superhero party featured new looks for old characters, including redesigned figures for Superman, Wonder Woman, Batman, and Aquaman. In addition to having their own comic books, the characters joined forces to fight crime in the Justice League of America, which was incredibly successful. In 1961 Marvel Comics took note and created its own team of super crime-busting heroes called the Fantastic Four. The characters, drawn by Marvel's Jack Kirby, forever changed the way superheroes were portrayed. The Fantastic Four consisted of Mister Fantastic, the Invisible Girl, the Human Torch, and the Thing. These were the first openly flawed superheroes—and they did not conceal their identities behind a mask. The Fantastic Four fought among themselves, held grudges, sought celebrity for their amazing deeds, and made major mistakes.

Kirby's imaginative artwork reimagined superheroes as more than crime busters. The Fantastic Four entered the realms of science fiction as they traveled far beyond the bonds of Earth to the mythological realm of Asgard and the parallel universe of the Negative Zone. The characters, themes, and story lines Kirby's artwork brought to life made the Fantastic Four an unexpected success and revived Marvel's financial fortunes.

Marvel continued to innovate throughout the 1960s as it introduced a wide range of now-immortal Kirby characters, including the Hulk, Thor, Ant-Man, and Black Panther, along with antagonists like Doctor Doom, Magneto, and Loki. In 1962 Marvel introduced one of its most popular characters, Spider-Man. Created by artist Steve Ditko, Spider-Man was the first teenage superhero—and kids loved him.

A New Realism

By the mid-1970s, American culture was changing. Slow economic growth and high rates of unemployment shook the nation. Factories shut down, and poverty rates skyrocketed. This new reality was reflected in comic books during an era referred to as the bronze age of comics, a period that ran from about 1971 to 1985. While superheroes continued to dominate, comic books began to reflect the gritty new realities. Artists and writers concocted dark plots that highlighted social issues such as pollution, poverty, racism, overpopulation, and drug addiction. The industry promoted these new story lines under the term *relevant comics*. DC characters Green Arrow and Green Lantern were at the forefront of this new style of comic. Their adventures took them across the country on quests to fix social problems. During this period readers were shocked to learn that the Green Arrow's clean-cut sidekick, Speedy, was a heroin addict. (Although the Comics Code banned portrayals of alcohol and drug use in any context, the CCA had changed the rules in 1973 to allow negative depictions of drugs.)

The reality-based stories in the Green Arrow and Green Lantern comics were also reflected in the artwork. Artist Neal Adams used a sophisticated art style called photorealism to depict the characters in both comics. As art reviewer John Strausbaugh explains, "Neal Adams brought to comics a realist's mastery of anatomical detail, facial expression and . . . precision [of movement] that caused a style revolution."[15]

The New Dark Ages

The power of the big-two comic book publishers continued well into the twenty-first century, a period that some call the dark age of comic books. That period, which began around 1985, was marked by a move toward darker, edgier, and more violent stories. In an effort to appeal to older readers, publishers began to ignore the restrictions of the Comics Code as traditional superheroes were transformed into antiheroes. These characters lacked qualities that would be considered heroic. Antiheroes were outcasts who could be mean, spiteful, and foolish. They preferred to work alone and rejected the help of others, even when they needed assistance. Dark-age villains were even worse as they twisted into characters who were meaner and creepier than ever.

The phrase *dark age of comic books* can be traced to several highly influential DC series. In 1986 Batman was reimagined as a middle-aged, bitter, sadistic alcoholic for the four-issue series *Batman: The Dark Knight Returns*. Frank Miller, the artist behind *The Dark Knight Returns*, attracted attention with his over-the-top, blood-spattered panels. Miller's generous use of gray and black in nearly every scene provided a brooding, ominous look that was seen as the epitome of the dark-age trend.

Although Miller violated tenets of the Comics Code and drew panels that dripped with gore, Alan Moore went even further. Moore was an English novelist, musician, and lover of the occult who created the grisly twelve-issue *Watchmen* series. *Watchmen* follows the crime-fighting escapades of Rorschach, a tormented vigilante wanted by the police. The multilayered story that Moore concocted with writer Dave Gibbons was more complex than anything previously seen in a comic book. *Watchmen* was a huge success and even achieved mainstream attention after the series

This panel from Watchmen *shows the dark character Rorschach. During the 1980s, comic books began featuring antiheroes, characters who were often troubled and who preferred to work alone.*

appeared in a graphic novel. *Time* magazine listed it as one of the one hundred greatest novels published since 1923—the only comic book to make it onto the list.

The success of *Watchmen* and *The Dark Knight Returns* showed that material aimed at adult readers had an enthusiastic audience. This inspired comic book store owner Mike Richardson to start Dark Horse Comics in 1986. Dark Horse was one of the first independent, or indie, publishers, and the company found immediate success with *Hellboy* and *Sin City*. Following this trend, seven respected Marvel artists founded their own company, Image Comics, in 1992.

Hollywood movie producers took note of the success of dark-age comic books. The 1989 film *Batman* became a blockbuster. Since that time the number of superhero movies and television shows seems to increase with every passing year. More than fifty shows based on comics appear annually in movie theaters or on television. In 2017 three of the top five highest-grossing films were based on superheroes, according to Box Office Mojo. In 2018 television viewers could tune into DC Comics' *Gotham*, *Lucifer*, *Preacher*, and *iZombie*, and its Arrowverse shows (*Arrow*, *Flash*, *Supergirl*, and *Legends of Tomorrow*). Marvel television programs included *Agents of S.H.I.E.L.D.*, *The Punisher*, *Runaways*, and others.

An Age of "Nerd Wonderment"

Among comic book fans there is little agreement as to when the dark age ended—or if it ever ended. But since the early 2000s, comics have diversified so much that they can no longer be categorized by any specific time period. Although Marvel and DC Comics continue to dominate the industry, independent artists have been publishing their work on the Internet and attracting readers through social media. Advanced technology has made it easier than ever to create comics as artists employ digital painting software and three-dimensional modeling programs to fill up their panels.

In the twenty-first century, comics reflect the view of a new generation of artists. Stories explore gender roles, race and discrimination, feminism, politics, and more. In 2010 Archie Comics introduced the first openly gay character, and in 2012 Marvel staged the first gay wedding between a superhero—Northstar—and his partner. In this modern era, Thor is a woman and Spider-Man is a black teen with Hispanic roots. As comic book reviewer Jamahl Johnson explains, "Comics have expanded into something without shape or borders—a nebulous mass of nerd wonderment."[16]

Although comics were once blamed for corrupting kids, they have grown into a cultural behemoth that fuels a multibillion-dollar industry. And from the innocent superheroes of the golden age, through the dark age, and into what might be called the independent age, comics continue to reflect the changing face of America and its values, culture, and history.

> "Comics have expanded into something without shape or borders—a nebulous mass of nerd wonderment."[16]
>
> —Jamahl Johnson, comic book reviewer

CHAPTER TWO

Artists of Influence

Superman, Batman, Spider-Man, Wonder Woman, and other famed comic book heroes have impacted pop culture throughout the world. Blockbuster films featuring superheroes are seen everywhere from the United States and Canada to China and the African nation of Zimbabwe. Images of comic book characters adorn clothing, toys, costumes, cups, posters, and hundreds of other items. While these comic book characters now enjoy global fame, they were all born in the United States where they first leapt to life on blank sheets of paper, the product of creative geniuses and skilled hands wielding pencils, pens, and paintbrushes.

The names of the artists who wielded those pens and paints are well-known to comics fans and comic book creators alike. Their unique characters and drawing styles influenced and shaped the ever-changing look and feel of comic books—and the comics industry itself. Illustrator and comic book historian Arlen Schumer believes that the work of the leading comic book artists rivals classical fine art styles of the past. Comic book art might not hang on the walls of famous art museums, but Schumer maintains that "just as art historians look back 500 years ago on the great Renaissance masters of the human figure like Michelangelo and Raphael, so too will art historians 500 years from now look back on the great masters of the human figure of our time, our great comic book artists like Jack Kirby, Neal Adams . . . Carmine Infantino, [and] Gil Kane."[17]

Jack Kirby, Creator of Captain America

Jack Kirby is often regarded as the industry's Michelangelo, an artist of unmatched creativity and influence. And it is said that Kirby drew more comic book pages in a year than most artists produced in a lifetime. While this might be an exaggeration, Kirby's impact on comic book art cannot be overstated. His creations—Thor, the Fantastic Four, Black Panther, and the Incredible Hulk, among others—are known worldwide to casual and devoted fans alike. And Kirby's artistic style has been imitated by countless artists since his characters first leapt to life.

Kirby grew up in the 1920s tracing comic strip characters featured in the Sunday funnies. In 1940 he created Captain America, a patriotic superhero draped in an American flag costume. One of the most enduring Captain America images shows him punching Nazi leader Adolf Hitler. The image of Captain America was unlike the era's dull, flat drawings of Superman and Batman. Kirby used irregularly shaped panels and distorted perspective to emphasize speed and heighten drama. He often showed Captain America flying straight at readers, who were suddenly face-to-face with their hero. As Kirby explains, "I tore my characters out of the panels. I made them jump all over the page."[18] The success of Captain America generated a multitude of imitators as artists struggled to match Kirby's groundbreaking visual techniques.

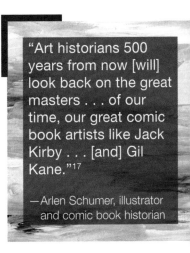

"Art historians 500 years from now [will] look back on the great masters . . . of our time, our great comic book artists like Jack Kirby . . . [and] Gil Kane."[17]

—Arlen Schumer, illustrator and comic book historian

By the 1960s Kirby was changing the way comic book stories were created. Previously, writers would take the lead, producing tightly scripted stories that included dialogue and brief scene descriptions. Artists would follow the script, creating drawings based on the writer's vision. But when Kirby worked with writer Stan Lee (who died in November 2018 at the age of ninety-five), the artist took the lead. The two would come up with a brief plot outline, and Kirby would break the story down into panels based on his vision of how the action should progress. Lee would then take the finished artwork and fill in the captions and dialogue.

This manner of producing comic books came to be known as the Marvel Method. Other Marvel artists were taught this process—and put it to use. The Marvel Method enhanced the role of the artists, shifting story development (including pacing and character creation) into their creative hands. The Marvel Method was not completely freeing. Artists were expected to match Kirby's style, as Green Lantern artist Gil Kane stated in 1985:

Jack's point of view and philosophy of drawing became the governing philosophy of the entire publishing company and, beyond the publishing company, of the entire field. . . . [Marvel took] Jack and [used] him as a primer. They would get artists . . . and they taught them the ABCs, which amounted to learning Jack Kirby. Jack was like the Holy Scripture and they simply had to follow him without deviation.[19]

Kirby's drawing style was unlike any other. He used abstract geometric patterns and stylized backgrounds in his art, and his characters had skin that gleamed like chrome. Explosions, smoke, clouds, ray-gun blasts, and cosmic energy from space radiated with pulsating dots called the Kirby Krackle. Artist Jeet Heer explains these mysterious dots, which crackled like lightning: "[The] Kirby Krackle, unleashed in scenes of energy or chaos, became a signature device, one that Kirby never explained but that, like so many of his quirks, compelled the eye."[20]

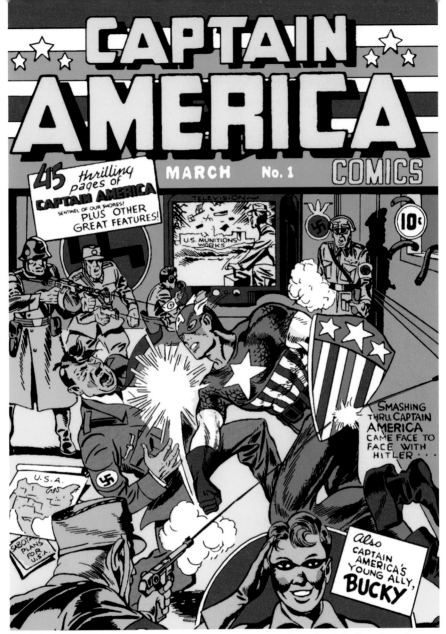

Comic book artist Jack Kirby created the patriotic superhero Captain America, shown here punching Nazi leader Adolf Hitler in the nose.

Superstar Penciller Jim Lee

Korean American artist Jim Lee is one of those who followed the Marvel Method when he began his career in 1987 as a freelance illustrator of titles like *Punisher: War Journal* and *Alpha Flight*. But Lee soon blazed his own trail at Marvel after he was selected

Jim Lee's Advice

Jim Lee is one of the most famous comic book artists of the modern era. In 2016 he offered this advice to aspiring comic book artists who want to create their own unique styles:

[Go] home and draw! It's like anything—there's a lot of work that goes into something before anyone will pay you for it. You can't rush it. You're not going to figure out how to create your style or your career in a month, or a few months. It's going to take years and years. You really have to pace yourself and make sure you don't burn out. There's never going to be a time where you come upon a look or a style and you think, "I've got it! I've found my finished look! I'm ready to be a published author or a published comic artist!". . . You keep learning and keep improving your craft. You want to make sure you have that momentum and enthusiasm throughout your entire career. If this is the road you want to go on, you're going to be running for a long, long time. If you commit to it fully, though, it really can be achievable.

Quoted in AMC, "Comic Book Men Q&A—Jim Lee," 2016. www.amc.com.

to illustrate issue number 248 of *Uncanny X-Men* in 1989. Lee employed a fine-line style of sketching that was an immediate hit with readers. His work on several subsequent issues led him to develop a legion of enthusiastic fans. With each issue of *Uncanny X-Men* outselling the one before, Lee quickly became the newest superstar comic book artist. In 1991 Lee launched the all new *X-Men* series that set new standards for the industry. Marvel released five different editions simultaneously. Each cover featured a different character, and all fit together to form a single large image. Fans purchased multiple copies of the comic to own each cover, pushing sales past 8 million copies. This made the first issue of *X-Men* the best-selling comic book of all time, according to the *Guinness Book of World Records*.

Despite his massive success, Lee felt he was not being properly rewarded for his talents. Although he was well-paid, Lee was a Marvel employee. He did not own the publishing rights to either the characters or the stories he created. This meant that Marvel was making much more money than Lee from his creations. In 1992 Lee teamed with some of the industry's hottest superstars, including Rob Liefeld (best known for his work on *X-Force)* and Todd McFarlane (*Spider-Man*), to found Image Comics. Since it was a creator-owned company, the artists would retain all profits generated from their work.

Comic book artist Jim Lee works in his office at DC Comics. As copublisher at DC Comics, Lee creates characters, contributes to ongoing series, and spearheads numerous new projects.

Lee created a superhero team called the WildCATs for his first Image Comic series. It was an immediate sensation, and early issues of the series sold over 1 million copies. This prompted Lee to spin off each character into its own series. In addition to creating his own comics, Lee's imprint, WildStorm Productions, published some of the best artists in the business. By the late 1990s, WildStorm was turning out a number of trendsetting new series, including *Sleeper*, which was a comic drawn by Sean Phillips that blended two genres: it featured a superhero who was also a secret agent.

During the early 2000s the success of WildStorm gave Lee the freedom to pursue new projects. He signed up with DC Comics to create new Batman and Superman titles, and in 2005 he launched the *All-Star Batman & Robin, the Boy Wonder* series. In 2010, eighteen years after leaving Marvel to start his own company, Lee was named copublisher of DC Comics. In this role, Lee became the public face of the company, giving interviews and appearing at San Diego's Comic-Con International and other conventions. In 2018 Lee was still considered one of the best pencillers in the business. He continued to create new characters, contribute to ongoing series, and spearhead numerous new projects.

Lee's finely detailed artwork spawned a legion of imitators as he rose from a struggling artist to the copublisher of the world's oldest established comic book company. Lee says those who dream of following his path to the top of the comic book industry should ask themselves, "What can I do that hasn't been done before? . . . Can I create something that adds to that mythology, that stands the test of time?"[21]

Becky Cloonan and Batman

Becky Cloonan was eleven years old when the first issue of *X-Men* was published. Cloonan, who had already discovered a love of drawing, later recalled that she was captivated by Jim Lee's work. Inspired by Lee, Cloonan decided she, too, would pursue

Compelled to Self-Publish

Becky Cloonan, who found success working for DC, self-publishes one comic book every year. "I feel like I'm compelled to keep making them," she says. The first of these, *Wolves*, came out in 2011, after she found herself waiting on the start of a new project for one of the major comic book publishers. Cloonan continues,

> I had a few months of scrambling to find another job. So I decided to self-publish something while I had this downtime. So I did that book *Wolves* and put it out myself. I sent it to all my friends, I would bring it to conventions, and the first print run was a thousand, and I think I sold out in like a month. It was ridiculous. So then I just reprinted it again, and I think until now, I've printed 7,000 copies of that book. It's been a few years. And then every year, I've done a new one. And then last year, my book *The Mire* won an Eisner Award for "Best Single Issue." So I was so honored because it was just a little thing that you put out yourself. You never think that it's going to reach that many people.

Quoted in Oliver Sava, "Becky Cloonan on Self-Publishing, Creative Obstacles, and *Gotham Academy*," AV Club, July 28, 2014. www.avclub.com.

a career as a comic book artist. Cloonan worked for both Marvel and DC. During her time with DC she even drew Batman—the first female artist to work on the stories of the caped crusader.

Although Cloonan loved *X-Men* and other superhero comics, she was also fascinated by Japanese comics called manga. The term *manga* is commonly interpreted to mean "whimsical pictures." Unlike extremely detailed drawings in American comics, manga characters look as if they were sketched rapidly in a spontaneous manner. As Asian art historians Jocelyn Bouquillard and Christophe Marquet explain, manga artists create "impromptu drawings done on the tide of inspiration, freely and with no sense of order."[22]

This sense of artistic freedom appealed to Cloonan, who decided to pursue comic book art at New York's School of Visual

Arts. During her college years, Cloonan was influenced by the movies of European filmmakers Fritz Lang and Carl Dreyer. Their Expressionist films, made during the 1920s and 1930s, were dark, disturbing, and gritty. As Cloonan explains, "Their films kind of blew my mind because, first of all, they're so creepy. But then on the other hand, their use of black and white was so stark and smooth. . . . When I started inking and drawing my own comics, I was taking a lot from that."[23]

Comic artist Becky Cloonan accepts the Eisner Award at the 2013 Comic-Con International Convention. In 2012, Cloonan became the first woman artist to draw an issue of Batman *for DC Comics.*

Cloonan self-published her first work in 1999. She created twelve minicomics, a genre so-named because only a small number of copies are produced. While working on her minicomics, Cloonan ignored her schoolwork, leading her to drop out in 2001 to pursue comic art full time. In 2003 she collaborated with writer Brian Wood to create the twelve-issue series *Demo*. Each issue featured young people with supernatural powers. *Demo* stories focused on emotions and relationships rather than clashes between heroes and villains. The manga influence can be clearly seen in *Demo*'s brilliant black-and-white artwork. The characters have large eyes, spiky hair, and button noses—features commonly seen in Japanese comic books.

Demo was well received by lovers of indie comics, as was Cloonan's manga-influenced graphic novel *East Coast Rising* (2006), which was about a group of punk rock pirates. For her work on both she was nominated for three prestigious Will Eisner Comic Industry Awards (commonly called Eisner Awards).

Despite critical acclaim for these projects, Cloonan did not achieve her big breakthrough until 2012, when DC Comics asked her to draw an issue of *Batman*. Cloonan was the first female artist to draw Batman in the character's seventy-two-year history, but she was unaware of this at the time:

> I didn't even know I was the first woman to draw *Batman* until after it happened. Thank God, because I don't know if I would have enjoyed that pressure. . . . After I found out . . . [I thought, that] can't be true. It's got to be someone else. But there had to be a first, and it happened to be me. . . . It's nice to be a part of history like that. But it's also a little sad that it's taken so long to happen.[24]

Batman brought Cloonan a level of recognition that she had not experienced before. Yet her main focus remains writing, illustrating, and self-publishing her original works: "Having something that's 100 percent me is very important. A lot of my stories are fantasies and medieval stuff, which are close to my heart."[25] In 2012 Cloonan won an Eisner Award for *The Mire*, the second book in a trilogy known as *By Chance or Providence*.

Cloonan works at her easel eight to nine hours a day and, unlike many of her colleagues, she does not use a computer. She sketches quickly with a pencil and finalizes each drawing with ink, completing around four pages a day. "I like having a big stack of paper when I'm finished,"[26] she says.

Cloonan remains dedicated to self-publishing a new comic each year even as she works on mainstream titles like *Gotham Academy* for DC and *The Punisher* for Marvel. In 2015 *Comic News* voted Cloonan number three of the top twenty-five female comic book artists of all time. As *Comic News* reviewer Brian Cronin explained, Cloonan's exceptional abilities provide inspiration to readers and indie comic book artists. She has "the ability to create real mood and atmosphere and emotional resonance through her imagery. A master of tension and pacing, Cloonan's work is magnificently difficult to put down thanks to her mastery of storytelling. It's all rather beautiful."[27]

The Saga of Fiona Staples

Canadian Fiona Staples is another comic book artist lauded for her ability to create arresting visuals that transport readers to other worlds. She creates complex sci-fi universes filled with characters whose faces express realistic emotions, even when they are spiderlike aliens with eight eyes. Reviewer John Martin has high praise for Staples's work: "Is Fiona Staples the greatest living artist in comics? I certainly [think] so."[28]

Staples's first major published work was the 2005 *Amphibious Nightmare*, which is known as a twenty-four-hour comic. These twenty-four-page works are written, drawn, and completed by a single person in a twenty-four-hour period. Staples's work attracted the attention of Jim Lee, who hired her in 2006 to work as one of several illustrators on the WildStorm graphic horror novel *Trick 'r Treat*. Staples's profile rose quickly as she attracted attention for her ability to tell tales through strong imagery. As Staples explains, "I had a real interest in visual story telling. When you read a book, you create images in your mind. . . . So I always enjoy doing drawings and creating representations of the things that I read."[29]

In 2011 Staples was recruited by DC Comics as a cover artist. She created covers for *DV8: Gods and Monsters*, *THUNDER Agents*, and *Archie*. This work earned Staples two Joe Shuster Awards (given out to Canadian comic book creators) for Outstanding Comic Book Cover Artist and Outstanding Comic Book Artist.

Although she enjoyed her work as a cover artist, Staples felt she was ready to tackle an ongoing series. In 2012 she read the script for *Saga*, written by Brian K. Vaughan, and was fascinated by the story. *Saga* combines space travel, science fiction, adventure, and fantasy. Sometimes the series is described as *Star Wars* meets *Lord of the Rings*. The story follows Alana and Marko, a couple of mixed-species aliens from two warring planets. They are on the run from authorities from both worlds with their newborn infant, Hazel. The story is narrated by the unseen, grown-up Hazel.

From the first six issues of volume one in 2012, reviewers were mesmerized by the depth of the *Saga* story and by Staples's depictions of the characters and action. Reviewer Kelly Thompson said she was "quite in love" with *Saga*:

> Staples' art . . . is simply a dream. Her characters are rendered starkly, exhibiting a loose energy, while her backgrounds are a subtle wash of soft colors and shapes. . . . Her character designs are inventive to the point of near-absurdity and I found myself cackling with delight at every new imagining. . . . Staples' art subverts everything so nothing is what it seems, or what you might guess it could be.[30]

Saga is populated by alien entities of various ages, genders, races, and sexual preferences. The comic has been lauded for its fascinating, fully realized female characters, including the trans-woman Petrichor, a transgender woman whom the ComicVerse website included in its article "The Dopest Women of Image Comics." In 2013 *Saga* won three Eisner Awards, including one for Best New Series. The Harvey Awards, named after comic book artist Harvey Kurtzman, gave the series six awards, including two to Staples for Best Artist and Best Colorist. Staples was nominated for two Joe Shuster Awards for Best Cover Artist and Best Artist. And the series won a British Fantasy Award and a Hugo Award, given for science fiction achievements.

Staples has continued to illustrate six-issue volumes of *Saga* each year, and by 2018 she had completed fifty-four issues. Although Hollywood executives have expressed interest in adapting *Saga* for film or television, Staples and Vaughan remain uninterested because they feel that the work would not translate well to either medium. As such, *Saga* has become one of the rare comic book sensations that found fame without the benefit of a blockbuster movie or television series. And there are doubtlessly dozens of aspiring comic book artists reading *Saga* today who will one day list Staples's work as their main motivation for picking up a tablet and filling in panels with lines, shading, and colors.

CHAPTER THREE

Creating a Following

In the past, the names of even the most prolific comic artists were unknown to the general public. While readers in the 1960s might have loved the Green Lantern and Captain Marvel, only the most hard-core devotees knew that Gil Kane was the genius behind the artwork. And most Marvel and DC Comics artists were even more obscure. In this era before the Internet and comic conventions there were few places where inkers, pencillers, and painters could meet fans or explain their artistic processes.

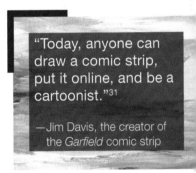

"Today, anyone can draw a comic strip, put it online, and be a cartoonist."[31]

—Jim Davis, the creator of the *Garfield* comic strip

Comic book artists of past decades would certainly be amazed if they could see the many ways their modern counterparts interact with the public and create dedicated followings. As *Garfield* creator Jim Davis notes, "Today, anyone can draw a comic strip, put it online, and be a cartoonist."[31] Davis is referring to artists who promote their comics through social media, comic book forums, chat groups, and comments sections. Some submit their panels to comic book review websites and register their comics with ranking websites where visitors vote on their favorite webcomics.

Internet resources are open to anyone and provide opportunities for new artists to compete with established favorites. But as Daniel Sharp, creator of the webcomic *The Demon Archives*, explains, self-promotion is never easy:

> If you make any creative endeavor and post it online, you often start off thinking that just by sheer virtue of how good it is, how much thought and care and effort you've put into it, everyone should like it and it should magically go viral and get popular. While sometimes that happens, normally it doesn't. There is SO much content out there already that you normally have to put a lot of work into promoting your stuff and getting the attention out.[32]

Social Media Mavens

In 2018 nearly 1.5 billion people—one out of every five people on Earth—had Facebook accounts. Around 800 million people used Instagram, and 335 million were signed up on Twitter. For self-promoting comic book artists who want to reach the largest audience, it is standard practice to regularly post on Facebook, Instagram, and Twitter. Artist Skottie Young, best known for his work on *The Wonderful World of Oz* and *Rocket Raccoon*, has around 240,000 followers on Instagram and 80,000 on Twitter. Young posts sketches of works in progress, covers of soon-to-be released comic books, pictures from comic conventions, and photos of his home studio. He also garners tens of thousands of likes from aspiring artists when he posts photos of his favorite pencils, ink, and lettering tools known as brush pens.

Social media can provide a lifeline to artists who live far from comic book industry hubs in New York and California. As Australia-based Wonder Woman artist Nicola Scott explains, "I get far fewer opportunities to meet or catch up with peers, mentors and fans. But through Twitter, Instagram and Facebook we can share in each other's triumphs and slumps, promote and share our work."[33]

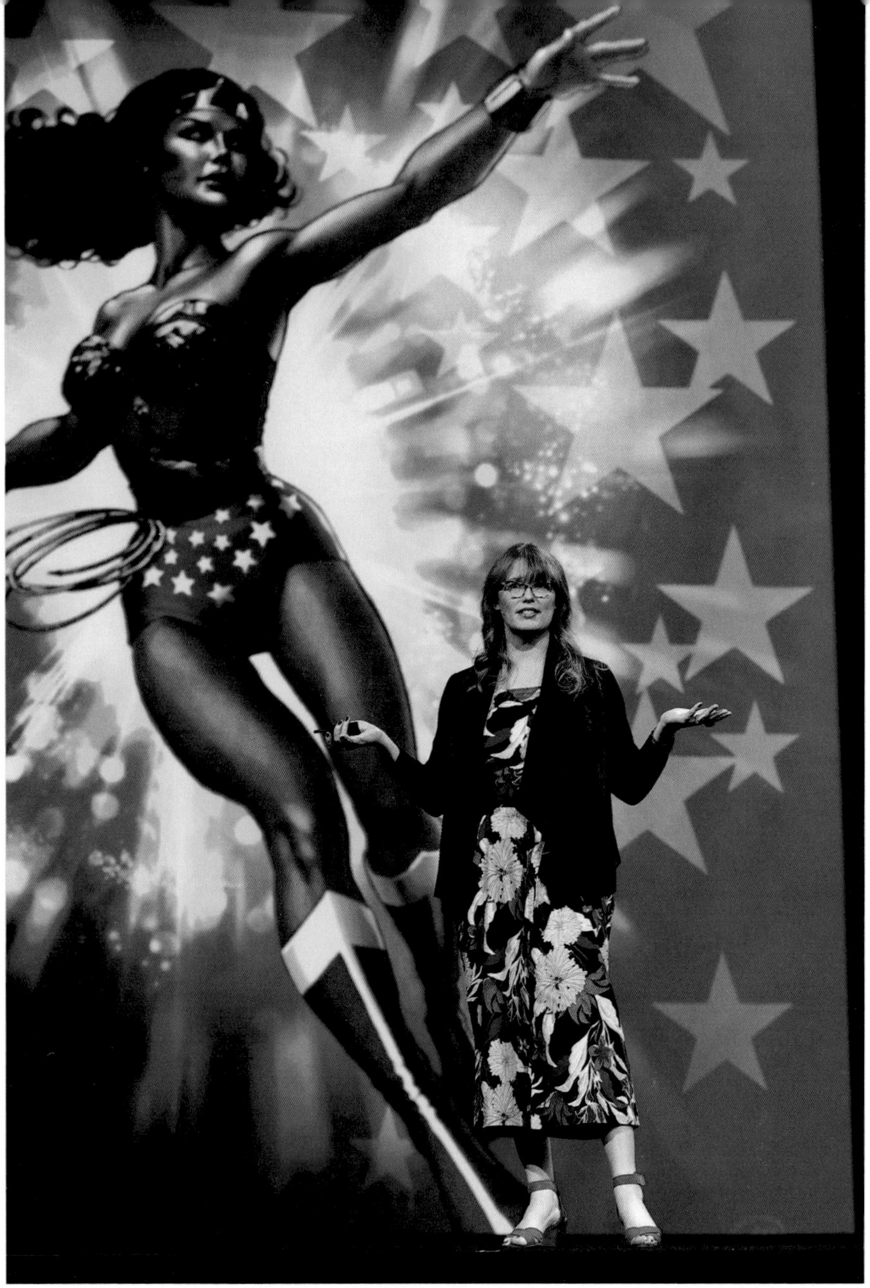

Based in Australia, Wonder Woman artist Nicola Scott says that Twitter, Instagram, and Facebook have been key to promoting her work and connecting with her fellow artists.

Social media is especially valuable to lesser-known comic artists who create webcomics. These artists promote their brands on personal websites, Facebook pages, Instagram, Twitter, and YouTube. They send out social media blasts to announce each new update, share tips, or simply converse with fans. Noah Bradley has over fourteen thousand fans who follow his webcomic *The Sin of Man*. According to Bradley, "I benefited from social media in building a fanbase for my work and connecting with fellow creators. I think I'd have had a harder time becoming as well known as I am now without it."[34]

> "I benefited from social media in building a fanbase for my work and connecting with fellow creators."[34]
>
> —Noah Bradley, webcomic artist

Mike Girardin, the creator of the webcomic *Antares Complex*, says the key to success on social media is to use identifying keywords and hashtags that can help readers find an artist's work: "It's good to sort out what keywords fit what you're posting: comic, scifi, indie-comic, female-protagonist, webcomic. Or what's happening in that specific piece: spaceship, sword fight, gunfight. It's important to lay that out so . . . search engines find your stuff if someone searches it."[35]

While there are positive aspects to promoting comics on social media, it can also be distracting to users who constantly check for likes or engage in Twitter wars with critics. Artists who wish to keep their social media focused on their professional accomplishments use scheduling tools like Hootsuite, TweetDeck, and Buffer. These apps automatically release content based on a predetermined timetable, allowing the artist to check in at a later date to deal with comments and replies.

Snotgirl and Social Media

Perhaps nothing better illustrates the connection between social media and comic books than *Snotgirl*, which debuted in 2016. *Snotgirl* is about green-haired fashion blogger and Instagram star "Snotty" Lottie Person, whose severe allergies cause her unending embarrassment. *Snotgirl* was conceived by Bryan Lee O'Malley (creator of the *Scott Pilgrim* graphic novels), who tapped artist Leslie Hung to illustrate the comic. Hung was an unknown artist who posted her illustrations to Twitter. O'Malley saw the pictures,

Comic Artists on YouTube

The video-sharing website YouTube has over 1.8 billion users every month. And countless comic book artists are using the site to promote their work and attract new fans. Comic book creator and writer Mark Crilley is one of the most successful YouTube comic artists. Crilley posted his first video in 2007 to promote his manga-style comic *Miki Falls*. Traffic to Crilley's site soared after he posted a clip that showed him drawing one of the *Miki Falls* characters and discussing his art techniques. Crilley began posting simple, unscripted weekly how-to videos that showcased his manga drawing style. Most featured a tight focus on his pencil and paper with an occasional time lapse that showed work being completed. Fans loved his videos; in 2009 Crilley posted "How to Draw a Realistic Eye," and by 2018 it had been viewed more than 29 million times.

With more than 2.5 million subscribers, Crilley's videos have generated 313 million views. He receives significant income from YouTube, and his graphic novel series *Brody's Ghost* is a best seller, due, in part, to his online popularity. As Crilley explains, "The YouTube thing is something that started very small and then somehow mushroomed into a big following."

Quoted in John Booth, "From Monty Python to *Mad* to Manga: An Interview with Mark Crilley," *Wired*, January 28, 2011. www.wired.com.

---

liked the way Hung drew female characters, and contacted her. O'Malley and Hung bonded over the fact that they both had severe allergies. They decided to collaborate on *Snotgirl*. According to Hung, "I thought it would be so funny if there was this character who was really perfect on the outside and then had, like, horrible allergies. We both have allergies, so we both found that whole snot aspect super hilarious."[36]

Snotgirl themes revolve around trends, memes, and the way people interact online and through text messages. As Hung explains, "The comic itself is very much about how technology and social media have become embedded in our everyday lives."[37] In a case of art imitating life, the Instagram photos Hung takes of her restaurant meals might also appear on Lottie's comic book Instagram feed. *Snotgirl*'s distinctive fashion style is inspired by fashion bloggers, designer Instagram feeds, and Pinterest posts that Hung follows. And the fashion focus led Hung to create a *Snotgirl* clothing line that she promotes on social media.

Reviews, Rankings, and Contests

While many contemporary comic book artists find social media the easiest way to promote their work, there are other methods that can be used to attract fans. Some set up link exchanges. This involves comic book artists placing links, or banner ads, on each other's websites to benefit both artists. Sharp provides an example:

> My friend Dan Butcher, creator of the excellent British superhero webcomic *Vanguard*, let me submit a [banner] ad of *The Demon Archives* which he put up on his site for a day during a break between chapters. He said some nice things and recommended his readers check me out. About 100 of them did, reading most of the archive, and more importantly, sticking around and visiting multiple times.[38]

Sharp repeated this process with twelve other comic book artists, which increased traffic to his site.

Sharp also submits *The Demon Archives* to comic book review sites like Webcomic Police to get feedback from readers. This process is not for everyone—readers tend to be either very supportive or extremely negative. However, the site attracts those who are very interested in reading webcomics by unknown artists and sometimes reviewers can be insightful.

Sites hosted by professional reviewers offer alternatives to those that allow readers to comment. The *Comics Journal* is an online review site that provides expert analysis of hundreds of webcomics. Sharp says artists who are reviewed on the site can expect a major increase in the number of visits to their websites.

Websites that feature podcast reviews are also helpful to webcomic artists. One such website, the Comics Alternative, is run by

Derek Royal and Andy Kunka, who claim to have "PhDs talking about comics."[39] Royal and Kunka have a weekly podcast in which they discuss and analyze the works of independent creators.

Although review sites can be very specific, ranking websites like TopWebComics (TWC) allow visitors to simply vote for their favorite comics. Webcomic artists who wish to participate in the ranking process provide a link to TWC on their websites. Readers are asked to click the link and cast a vote for the artist's comic. It only takes around forty votes to get a comic in the TWC Top 100, and artists can attract over five hundred new readers to their sites every month if they achieve high rankings on the TWC.

The TWC art contest is another way a comic book artist can attract fans. Entering a contest requires labor on the artist's part but does not cost anything. All participants have their webcomic featured on TWC's front page, and winners receive prizes and free advertising worth several hundred dollars. As Sharp writes, the contest "can draw eyes from the contest page to you and your work. The prizes are also . . . quite excellent. . . . Definitely worth it."[40]

Self-Publishing

Webcomics have flourished over the years because they offer an alternative way for comic artists to attract an audience. Marvel and DC Comics have controlled around three-quarters of the comic book industry for decades and tightly restrict what they publish. Another huge company, Diamond Comic Distributors, controls most of the distribution market, making it extremely difficult for independent artists to get their products on the shelves of comic book stores. This has led a number of up-and-coming comic artists to self-publish their work and sell it online.

Comic artist Charlie "Spike" Trotman found success by setting up the publishing company Iron Circus Comics. Trotman began her career in 2005 with the online publication of her webcomic *Templar, Arizona*, which is about a fictional town that exists in an alternate universe. Few artists earn money directly from their

Comic Book Forums

Webcomic artists have found that they can grow their fan base by reviewing and commenting on the works of others in webcomic forums like Smack Jeeves, ComicFury, and Comic Genesis. Forums provide space for artists and fans to discuss their comics through posted messages. Artists can contribute samples of their work or find writers and other artists for collaboration. Forums also offer art tutorials and techniques and advice about the comic book business. Community forums offer space for reader reviews, discussions of specific topics, such as manga or monsters, and news about meet ups, conventions, and other social gatherings.

Forums are easy to join, and artists can include banners in their signatures that link to their webcomics. Blogger LibertyCabbage provides advice to webcomic artists hoping to expand their following:

> Talk with people, be interesting, and be a part of the community; every post you make, even if it isn't related to comics, is helping to promote your webcomic because of the link in your signature. It's also a great way to network with other creators, get a better understanding of making comics, and get feedback from your peers. Each of these forums also has a "self-promotion" section where creators can advertise their webcomics.

LibertyCabbage, "10 Free and Effective Ways to Promote Your Webcomic," Webcomic Police, 2017. www.webcomicpolice.com.

webcomics, but Trotman was able to continue her work by appealing to her followers. She put a digital "tip jar" link next to the *Templar, Arizona* comic that contained a little thermometer. Beneath the link Trotman posted a message that told readers that for every $200 Trotman was able to raise, she would create an additional *Templar* episode. Trotman was shocked by the response. So many fans took her up on her challenge that she was able to set up a system for preordering published versions of *Templar*. Trotman collected money from customers for several months, until she had enough funds to print the comic books and ship them from her Chicago studio.

Trotman was also an early adopter of Kickstarter. In 2009 she used the crowdfunding site to raise money for the creation of a print version of *Templar*. The campaign was a huge success; she exceeded her fund-raising goal by about $20,000. By 2018 she had raised over $1 million on Kickstarter thanks to a fast-expanding group of devoted fans. She used the money to publish her own work and to promote creator-owned works like E.K. Weaver's *The Less than Epic Adventures of TJ and Amal* and Sophie Campbell's *Shadoweyes*.

Self-publishing is not easy. Those who work for large publishers have teams of artists who perform different tasks. Self-published artists often write their stories, draw the cover and every panel, and create all the graphics and lettering. In addition, they need to continually maintain their social media accounts. As Trotman explains, "That means answering email four hours a day. I can't be *too* put out about it; this is something I worked for, so clearly I want it. . . . [And] it's comforting that this isn't all empty labor. It produces amazing things."[41]

One of the amazing things Trotman refers to is her growing fan base, which funds new releases every year. And she has a secondary business. So many people asked Trotman about her success that she began selling a how-to comic that provides tips to artists who want to self-publish their work.

Attracting Like-Minded Fans

Trotman says she was originally motivated to self-publish because she wanted to see comics that no one else was making. According to comics journalist Caitlin Rosberg, "It's a theme that comes up time and time again when you talk to people who publish their own work, either online or physically. Almost every single person expresses frustration with what's offered by larger publishers and recounts the moment when they decided to start making the comics themselves, if they couldn't just go to their local comic shop and buy them."[42]

The comic artist Sfé R. Monster felt this way. He wanted to read comics that focused on what he calls queer science fiction (sci-fi) and fantasy, but he could not find them in his hometown of Halifax, Nova Scotia. Monster addressed the issue in a 2015 tweet: "I think someone should make an anthology of queer, LGBT sci-fi/fantasy stories because I want to be in it!"[43] He was immediately flooded with messages telling him to do it himself.

While some of the tweets were snarky, the responses motivated Monster to crowdsource a project on Kickstarter with the goal of publishing a queer comic anthology called *Beyond*. More than twenty-five hundred people responded, and Monster raised $80,000, far more than his original goal. To create the anthology, Monster put out an open call to comic book artists for submissions, expecting about thirty proposals. More than 240 artists responded, including *Saga* artist superstar Fiona Staples.

In 2017 Monster put out a call to artists for a second anthology of *Beyond* and received 480 submissions. And by this time, he was already planning the third volume. In addition to self-publishing anthologies, Monster writes and draws a weekly webcomic, *Eth's Skin*, about mermaids and sea monsters in British Columbia. Like Trotman, Monster struggles to balance his creative work with the demands of the self-publishing business. He deals with taxes and budgets, reads through submissions, and works to coordinate the output of thirty comic book artists for each anthology. Sometimes, when Monster needs advice, he turns to an online community of self-published comic book artists who discuss their successes and failures. As Rosberg explains, "The greatest tool in any self-publisher's arsenal isn't Kickstarter or software, it's the ability to network and connect with other people that can help."[44]

"The greatest tool in any self-publisher's arsenal isn't Kickstarter or software, it's the ability to network and connect with other people that can help."[44]

—Caitlin Rosberg, comics journalist

48

The Convention Scene

Comic book artists seeking more readers often attend annual events such as the Small Press Expo (SPX) in Bethesda, Maryland. The SPX is dedicated to independent comic book artists and writers and attracts around four thousand comic book enthusiasts each year. The event features a huge exhibit floor packed with creators selling indie comics. Some comic books are published by professionals, others are simply photocopied and stapled together. There are panel discussions featuring comic book creators, and the organization presents outstanding artists with Ignatz Awards, named for a character in the classic Krazy Kat comic strip.

Many creators who set up tables at the relatively small SPX are driven by a passion for what they do and are drawn to the event to connect with fans. As comic artist Whit Taylor explains, "It's not just a way to sell comics or buy comics. It's also a social event. . . [a chance to] meet new people both during the show and after the show and that's kind of the most meaningful part to me."[45]

Many who attend the SPX are not necessarily looking for mainstream success, but some have found it. Major entertainment companies, including the Cartoon Network and Disney, send talent scouts to the expo, and a few indie comic book artists have signed major deals. Rebecca Sugar began selling her *Steven Universe* comic books at the convention and went on to create the animated *Steven Universe* television series on the Cartoon Network. Lisa Hanawalt, whose work can be seen on the animated Netflix series *Bojack Horseman*, was the first woman to win the SPX Ignatz Award for Outstanding Comic in 2010.

While the SPX continues to grow, its attendance numbers cannot compare to San Diego's Comic-Con International. Widely known as Comic-Con, the annual event attracts up to 167,000 attendees. Although major entertainment companies

The Cartoon Network's series Steven Universe *originated from comic books of the same title, created by artist Rebecca Sugar.*

and publishers dominate Comic-Con, some indie artists exhibit their work in an area called Artists' Alley.

San Diego's Comic-Con is the largest comic book festival in the world and there are dozens of smaller comic conventions held in cities throughout North America, Europe, and elsewhere. Comic book creators attract new fans at these conventions in a number of ways. In addition to selling their comics and related merchandise, they hand out free items like sketches, bookmarks, and stickers. Comic artists speak on panels and hold workshops for aspiring artists. Comic book creator Kamikaze explains his convention tactics: "Your main goal isn't to get [attendees] to BUY it's to get them to give you ongoing support. . . . Focus on getting readers, because readers love your work, want to see more and will ultimately support you more."[46]

As Kamikaze makes clear, creating a following requires patience and dedication. Whether they are using conventions or social media, successful comic book artists need business and sales skills equal to their creative talents. Although Facebook can act as a launching pad for a webcomic artist, it is only the first step in a long journey through crowdsourcing, self-publishing, comic book conventions, and other methods that create a dedicated following of fans.

CHAPTER FOUR

Graphic Novels Pushing Boundaries

Celebrated artist Will Eisner was always a rebel who challenged the norms that defined comic books. In his 1940s comic strip *The Spirit*, he incorporated the bold imagery, vivid colors, and exaggerated shapes of the Romantic and Expressionist periods. This style represented a marked difference from the drab colors and dull drawings seen in Superman and most other mid-twentieth-century comics. In 1978 Eisner took comics in an entirely new direction with the publication of the graphic novel *A Contract with God and Other Tenement Stories*. Unlike the comic books of the time, whose stories mostly revolved around superheroes and villains, Eisner's graphic novel featured four stories that touched on his upbringing in the Bronx in New York City during the 1930s.

In *A Contract with God*, Eisner sought to create a work of literature, which can be defined as a written work of lasting artistic merit. Eisner created long, character-driven stories set on a fictional street he called Dropsie Avenue. Eisner described heartbreak, hope, corruption, and crime as it was experienced by real people living through economic turmoil caused by the Great Depression.

Although the term *graphic novel* was first used in 1964, *A Contract with God* has come to define the form. While a 28-page comic book might be seen as an episode of a television show in which all the problems are solved in thirty minutes, graphic novels, which can run to 130 pages, are comparable to full-length feature films in which stories unfold at a leisurely pace. In *A Contract with God*, Eisner's intricate stories are told with detailed, sepia-colored drawings that fill entire pages. Some pages feature several drawings artfully blended without the use of panels. Large blocks of text that narrate the story are artfully incorporated into the scenes. *A Contract with God* is also distinguished by its physical form. Comic books are printed on cheap pulp paper held together with staples. *A Contract with God* was a book, printed

Will Eisner works at his drawing board in his Florida studio in 1998. Eisner's 1978 work, A Contract with God and Other Tenement Stories, *came to define the graphic novel art form.*

on quality paper stock with a thick cover. And like a book, Eisner's graphic novel was initially sold in bookstores rather than in comic book shops.

A Contract with God was not a commercial success when it was initially released, but early reviews in publications such as the Comics Journal called the work a masterpiece. A Contract with God also had a major impact on the creative community as comic artists and reviews began referring to Eisner as the father of the graphic novel. Eisner continued his pioneering work on two more graphic novels, A Life Force and Dropsie Avenue, set in the tenements of the Bronx. The three books are known as the Contract with God trilogy and have been credited with popularizing graphic novels. As comics scholar Caitlin McCabe writes, "The mark that Eisner left on the form has without a doubt opened the door for a longer and more literary form of comics storytelling that has been adopted by creators around the world."[47] Eisner went on to create more than twenty graphic novels. In 2002, at the age of eighty-five, Eisner published a graphic novel of Herman Melville's 1851 classic Moby-Dick.

"[Will Eisner] opened the door for a longer and more literary form of comics storytelling that has been adopted by creators around the world."[47]

—Caitlin McCabe, comics scholar

Making Graphic Novels Respectable

The same year Eisner released A Contract with God, Marvel published The Silver Surfer by Stan Lee and Jack Kirby. This was Marvel's first graphic novel and the first to feature a superhero. Although Eisner believed that comics could be a serious literary art form, reviewers disagreed, pointing to The Silver Surfer as proof that graphic novels were mainly long-form comic books aimed at kids.

Graphic novels were largely ignored by book reviewers until 1986, when comic book artist Art Spiegelman published the first book of his two-part graphic novel Maus: A Survivor's Tale.

Librarians Embrace Graphic Novels

Perhaps no one embraced this idea of graphic novels as literature more readily than librarians. The graphic novel category became the fastest-growing section in the library after the 2002 American Library Association convention in Atlanta. A panel discussion featuring *Maus* creator Art Spiegelman, superstar writer Neil Gaiman (*Sandman*), and *Bone* creator Jeff Smith introduced graphic novels to librarians who were unfamiliar with them. As Gaiman later recalled,

> Librarians were getting pressures from their readers. The librarian knew that graphic novels . . . were popular and they wanted to know what they were. So they got [us] to tell them what we thought they should know. And the libraries have started ordering the books. . . . The battle to get comics taken seriously and to become part of the world had just been won at that moment.

Quoted in David Serchay, "The Day Comics Won," Diamond Bookshelf, October 13, 2018. www.diamond bookshelf.com.

The graphic novel tells the story of Spiegelman's father, Vladek, a Jew who lived in Poland during the Holocaust—when 6 million European Jews were systematically murdered by the Nazis. Vladek survived two years in the notorious Auschwitz death camp in Poland. The black-and-white panels of *Maus* move back and forth between Vladek's experiences during the 1940s and his life in Queens, New York, during the 1980s. All of the characters are represented as animals: the Jews are mice, the Germans are cats, the Americans are dogs, and the Poles are pigs. Spiegelman appears in a parallel story as a cartoonist who describes his strained relationship with his father, who is portrayed as an irritable, fearful man.

Describing the horrors of the Holocaust was not an easy task. Spiegelman began work on the graphic novel in 1980, and it took six years to complete the first six chapters. That work paid off. When the first volume, *Maus: A Survivor's Tale*, was released in 1986, the graphic novel won wide praise from reviewers at the nation's most respected publications, including the *New York Times* and *Washington Post*. When the second volume of the work, *And Here My Troubles Began*, was published in 1991, the critical acclaim further heightened public exposure to this new, serious style of graphic novel.

The positive publicity surrounding *Maus* helped change the public's view of graphic novels. As artist and comic book historian Robert C. Harvey explains, "The work demonstrates . . . that the medium [the graphic novel] is capable of achieving the status of serious literature, that it can tell serious stories with serious purposes in mind. In this alone, Spiegelman did his part to elevate the medium into the realm of respectability."[48] In 1992 *Maus* became the first graphic novel to win a Pulitzer Prize special award in letters. Spiegelman's book also won numerous comic book awards.

In addition to making graphic novels respectable, *Maus* influenced a generation of comic book creators. As Chris Ware, the creator of *Jimmy Corrigan: The Smartest Kid on Earth* and *Building Stories* explained in 2016, "Probably more than any other single comic, it made me see not only the potential for complex, moving and intelligent storytelling in comics, but also galvanized my own resolve to become a graphic novelist."[49] *Maus* also helped change the way educators viewed graphic novels. Perhaps no one embraced this idea more readily than librarians who viewed graphic novels as a way to get students interested in reading. As library shelves filled with graphic novels, comic book creators responded with a flood of award-winning books that accelerated the trend toward wider acceptance.

Bringing History Alive

One of the most celebrated graphic novels of the 2000s, *Persepolis* by Marjane Satrapi, has often been compared to *Maus*. Both stories were illustrated in a heavy black-and-white drawing style and both provided eyewitness views of historical events. *Persepolis*, published in English in two parts between 2003 and 2004, is autobiographical. It describes Satrapi's childhood in Iran

In her graphic novel, Persepolis, artist Marjane Satrapi describes how friends and family members suffered persecution under Iran's fundamentalist regime after the Islamic Revolution in 1979.

during the Islamic Revolution that began in 1979. Satrapi uses a mix of scornful humor and sadness to describe the brutality of the strict fundamentalist regime that persecuted, arrested, and executed her family members and friends. The graphic novel moves through the years as Satrapi leaves Iran to attend school in Vienna, Austria.

Persepolis set the tone for graphic novels that reflect both history and life from the perspective of a young person. Her personalized story was credited with bringing the event to life for readers who might have only read newspaper accounts or historical overviews. *Persepolis* eventually sold over 1.5 million copies worldwide and was adapted as an animated film in 2007.

Marching Through History

Another prime example of a graphic novel that gives a new relevance to historical events was written by civil rights icon and US congressman John Lewis. The *March* trilogy covers the civil rights movement of the early 1960s. *March: Book One*, published in 2013, written by Lewis and illustrated by award-winning graphic novelist Nate Powell, recalls Lewis's teenage years in rural Alabama and his experiences with segregation and racism. The graphic novel explores Lewis's meetings with civil rights leaders and his clashes with police while participating in sit-ins at lunch counters. Powell's artwork puts readers into the scene, where they can relive the turbulent era. As comic book reviewer Meryl Jaffe writes,

> Powell's black and white images empower viewers to comprehend those volatile times as we intimately view their unfolding events. Powell deftly uses contrast . . . sharp angles, and lettering to relay violent emotions. . . . There are beautiful wide-angle shots establishing historic locations, and sharp, angular lines . . . to relate Lewis' personal turmoil and the drama of these famous and infamous events.[50]

The dramatic artistic tone continues through the other two volumes of the series, *March: Book Two* and *March: Book Three*. In 2016 the trilogy occupied the top three spots on the *New York Times* best-seller list for graphic books and won the 2016 National Book Award for young people's literature. In 2018 Lewis published a follow-up to *March* called *Run: Book One*, which follows him through the civil rights movement of the late 1960s.

"Shades of Grey"

March and *Persepolis* are part of a continuing trend to tell the authentic stories of real people from diverse backgrounds. This movement has seen graphic novel creators addressing serious social problems. Acclaimed artist and illustrator Jarrett J. Krosoczka is best known for his Lunch Lady series of graphic novels (2009–2014). These stories depict a school cafeteria worker who is a secret crime fighter. But in 2018 Krosoczka decided to tackle a much more serious topic in the graphic memoir *Hey, Kiddo*, which describes his struggle as the son of a heroin-addicted mother. *Hey, Kiddo* depicts Krosoczka during the years he was raised by his grandparents as his mother cycled in and out of his life. At that time, the main bright spot in his life was creating art, and part of the story shows Krosoczka developing into an artist. Krosoczka recalls that

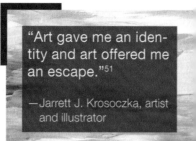

"art gave me an identity and art offered me an escape." While Krosoczka's artwork is known to be bright and colorful, *Hey, Kiddo* is drawn in shades of burnt orange and gray. As Krosoczka explains, "I wanted the greyscales to be symbolic of my [realization] that life and people cannot be measured in black and white, rather varying shades of grey."[51]

Hey, Kiddo is one of a growing number of young adult graphic novels exploring issues of addiction. Cecilia Galante's 2018 *Strays Like Us* depicts a character placed in a foster home because her mother was arrested for stealing prescription painkillers. Jennifer and Matthew Holm's graphic novel *Swing It, Sunny* is about a girl whose older brother is struggling with addiction. Krosoczka comments on the positive aspects of this storytelling trend: "Kids need books like this so that they feel less alone."[52]

Tillie Walden's Worlds

Many painful adolescent emotions are related to sexual orientation, a fact that motivated graphic novelist Tillie Walden to create autobiographical stories for young adults. Walden attracted great acclaim for her sensitive portrayal of growing up gay in the world of competitive figure skating. Her 2017 memoir *Spinning* was originally a short comic book but grew into a four-hundred-page graphic novel that depicted her memories of skating, rivalries, romance, bullying, and trauma. Walden became disillusioned by the culture surrounding figure skating at the same time she discovered her talents as an artist. She gave up the sport to concentrate on comics.

Artist Tillie Walden, in her graphic novel On a Sunbeam, *explores LGBTQ life in outer space.*

Walden was only twenty-one when *Spinning* was published. Most people do not write memoirs at that age, but her story resonated with reviewers. Walden won an Eisner Award for *Spinning*, which made her the youngest person to ever win that prestigious award.

In Walden's subsequent graphic novel, *On a Sunbeam*, the artist leaves Earth to explore LGBTQ life in outer space. *On a Sunbeam* portrays a woman named Mia in a tricked-out spaceship who travels the universe to repair old buildings while also searching for Grace, her lost love. Mia and her all-female crew experience excitement, boredom, love, loss, and loneliness as they travel through space. The story breaks many conventions found in science fiction. Characters breathe in space and the universe is filled with big trees and ancient buildings. But as Walden says, "It's my world. My rules."[53]

Walden uses artwork to help tell the tale with a "sunset palette of oranges, yellows, and purples, with the occasional dusky blue,"[54] according to reviewer Rowan Hisayo Buchanan. The main story of *On a Sunbeam* is told in shades of purple. The flashback scenes are dominated by shades of blue. Walden skillfully uses her black ink pen to create incredibly detailed fantasy worlds with fish-shaped spaceships, magical forests, and haunted gothic cities floating in deep space. Perspective is used as a tool to illustrate emotions. Scenes are slightly tilted and elongated from below to evoke feelings of awe. Lone characters are shown from high above in a way that makes them seem isolated and insignificant. Trees and other background elements are accented in amber and shades of red to give scenes added depth.

On a Sunbeam first appeared as a webcomic. After it was nominated for the Eisner Award for Best Digital Comic in 2017, Walden was motivated to expand the story into a five-hundred-page graphic novel. Having published five graphic novels before the age of twenty-two, Walden's worlds and rules will undoubtedly continue to entertain and mystify readers.

Kamala Khan Is a Marvel

As artists like Walden upend graphic novel traditions with new story lines and characters, other artists are challenging those conventions by revitalizing well-established characters and themes. Ms. Marvel, the female counterpart to Captain Marvel, was introduced to the public in 1968, but the character appeared only sporadically over the decades. In 2014 Ms. Marvel took on a new form when creator Sana Amanat, writer G. Willow Wilson, and artist Adrian Alphona reintroduced the character as Kamala Khan, a sixteen-year-old kid from New Jersey who is a Muslim of Pakistani descent.

In the graphic novel *Ms. Marvel, Volume 1: No Normal*, Kamala is a funny, nerdy teenager who is exposed to a mysterious alien substance, Terrigen Mist, which gives her shape-shifting abilities. She takes on the name Ms. Marvel and sets out to fight supervillains even as she struggles to please her conservative family. Initially, the idea of a female Muslim superhero seemed controversial. Some commentators expected the character to tackle sensitive issues of politics, gender, and religion. But as Marvel's editor in chief, Axel Alonso, explains, the comic was not created to make a political statement. Kamala Kahn, he says, is "a teenager and she's struggling to find her own path. She's imbued with great power and she learns the responsibility that comes with it. That's a universal story. The fact that she's female and first generation American, continuously struggling with the values and authority of her parents, gives the story extra nuance, but it's a universal human story."[55]

The audience for graphic novels seemed to agree that the character was relatable, and the reaction to Ms. Marvel was overwhelmingly positive. Kamala Khan quickly became one of the company's most popular new characters. Alphona's flair for character design was extolled by fans who appreciated Kamala's facial expressions as she morphs into Ms. Marvel. After she yells "Transform!" her chin juts out, her eyes squeeze shut, and she expresses extreme resolve. When returning to her normal shape, Ms. Marvel instructs her limbs to "disembiggen" with a scowl that turns into a satisfied smile. Reviewer Aditi Shiva describes how Alphona's artwork adds to Kamala's personality:

> One moment she's rolling her eyes at her melodramatic older brother, giving him some merciless side-eye, the next she's all eyes-wide-open as she learns her parents

know she snuck out of the house. And then there's Kamala's gorgeously lively hair, which always seems to be protesting, or enthusing, together with her. . . . Right down to Kamala's body language, Alphona does a great job of making her responses realistic and believable.[56]

Ms. Marvel, Volume 1: No Normal was the best-selling graphic novel upon its release in October 2014, and the book won the Hugo Award for Best Graphic Story in 2015. The follow-up book, *Ms. Marvel, Volume 2: Generation Why*, debuted in 2015 at number four on the *New York Times* best-seller list of graphic books. Buoyed by the success, Marvel has published a new Kamala Khan graphic novel every year. And Kamala was just one Marvel character to challenge accepted norms. In the last few years, the company has introduced a diverse group of black, Hispanic,

Chris Ware's *Building Stories*

Chris Ware's attention to detail and realistic, meticulous drawing style is often compared to early twentieth-century comic strips like *Little Nemo* and *Gasoline Alley*. After reading Art Spiegelman's graphic novel *Maus* during the mid-1980s, Ware decided to become a graphic novelist, using his experiences growing up in Omaha, Nebraska, to inform his stories. Ware's 2000 graphic novel *Jimmy Corrigan: The Smartest Kid on Earth* was lauded by critics for its sensitive character portraits. But Ware's award-winning 2012 work, *Building Stories*, is perhaps the most unusual graphic novel ever produced.

Building Stories is a box set of fourteen different items that tell stories about people living in a three-story Chicago apartment building. One of the main characters is the apartment building itself, which expresses its thoughts in cursive lettering. The *Building Stories* box set includes several hardbound graphic novels, three comic books, various-sized pamphlets and leaflets, a flip book, a poster, a game board with no playing pieces, and several large broadsheet comic strip sections similar to the Sunday funnies sold during the late 1930s. Ware began work on *Building Stories* in 2002, and it took him a decade to complete. The work has been described as a masterpiece by reviewers and has won numerous book and comics awards.

Asian American, and female superheroes. But as Amanat says, "We've accomplished quite a bit, but we have a ways to go. We have to promote the diverse characters across the platforms in [graphic novels and other] formats. We are bringing in creators of different backgrounds to tell stories from a different point of view, particularly the minority characters."[57]

New Narratives

Long before graphic novels featured a diverse cast of characters, comic books mirrored cultural shifts and changing attitudes. But the rising popularity of graphic novels as literature coincided with changing demographics. Nearly 50 million immigrants have arrived in the United States since *A Contract with God* was first published, and Americans are more racially and ethnically diverse than ever before. This trend is reflected in numerous coming-of-age graphic novels written from the perspective of kids from China, India, Africa, and the Middle East. Additionally, social issues that were once kept out of sight, such as sexual orientation, drug addiction, and depression, are now openly discussed in graphic novels.

Whatever the subject might be, it is a sure bet that there is a graphic novel to cover it. From gay figure skaters to Muslim superheroes, graphic novels are blending beautiful artwork with moving stories. New worlds await between the covers of graphic novels that are focusing on the joys, confusion, and hardships of life in ways countless readers can understand.

$\mathcal{S}$OURCE NOTES

Introduction: The Changing Culture of Comic Books

1. David Youngquist, "Comic Books: Not Just for Kids Anymore," LinkedIn, March 6, 2015. www.linkedin.com.
2. Youngquist, "Comic Books."
3. Quoted in Jeremy Berlin, "Comics Color Outside the Lines, Drawing a Diverse Cast of Heroes," *National Geographic*, June 2017. www.nationalgeographic.com.
4. Quoted in Erin Maxwell, "Women Quietly Become a Force in Comic Book World," *Variety*, October 6, 2015. https://variety.com.
5. Quoted in Samara Lynn, "The Business of Black Comic Books," *Black Enterprise*, February 18, 2018. www.blackenterprise.com.

Chapter One: A Brief History of Comic Art

6. Quoted in Coulton Waugh, *The Comics*. New York: Macmillan, 1991, p. 6.
7. Quoted in Frederik L. Schodt, *Manga! Manga! The World of Japanese Comics*. Tokyo: Kodansha, 1997, p. 43.
8. Robert Petersen, *Comics, Manga, and Graphic Novels*. Santa Barbara, CA: Praeger, 2011, p. 142.
9. Fred Van Lente and Ryan Dunlavey, *The Comic Book History of Comics*. San Diego: IDW, 2012, p. 37.
10. William Moulton Marston, "Why 100,000,000 Americans Read Comics," *American Scholar*, Winter: 1943–44; reprinted June 8, 2017. https://theamericanscholar.org.
11. Petersen, *Comics, Manga, and Graphic Novels*, p. 149.
12. Lente and Dunlavey, *The Comic Book History of Comics*, p. 92.
13. Arlen Schumer, *The Silver Age of Comic Book Art*. Bloomington, IN: Archway, 2015, pp. 8–9.

14. Quoted in Carmine Infantino and David Spurlock, *The Amazing World of Carmine Infantino: An Autobiography*. Lebanon, NJ: Vanguard, 2001, p. 54.
15. John Strausbaugh, "60's Comics: Gloomy, Seedy, and Superior," *New York Times*, December 14, 2003. www.nytimes.com.
16. Jamahl Johnson, "The Amazing Stylistic History of Comic Books," *Creative Edge* (blog), 99Designs, 2016. https://99designs.com.

Chapter Two: Artists of Influence

17. Arlen Schumer, "Art & Comic Book Art," 13th Dimension, March 23, 2015. https://13thdimension.com.
18. Quoted in Robert C. Harvey, *The Art of the Comic Book*. Jackson: University Press of Mississippi, 1996, p. 33.
19. Quoted in Joe Sergi, *The Law for Comic Book Creators: Essential Concepts and Applications*. Jefferson, NC: McFarland, p. 179.
20. Jeet Heer, "Jack Kirby, the Unknown King," *New Republic*, August 28, 2017. https://newrepublic.com.
21. Quoted in AMC, "Comic Book Men Q&A—Jim Lee," 2016. www.amc.com.
22. Jocelyn Bouquillard and Christophe Marquet, *Hokusai: The First Manga Master*. New York: Abrams, 2007, p. 9.
23. Quoted in Oliver Sava, "Becky Cloonan on Self-Publishing, Creative Obstacles, and *Gotham Academy*," AV Club, July 28, 2014. www.avclub.com.
24. Quoted in Sava, "Becky Cloonan on Self-Publishing, Creative Obstacles, and *Gotham Academy*."
25. Quoted in Douglas Wolk, "Meet the First Female Comic Book Artist to Draw Batman," Oprah.com, 2013. www.oprah.com.
26. Quoted in Wolk, "Meet the First Female Comic Book Artist to Draw Batman."
27. Brian Cronin, "Top 25 Female Comic Book Artists #3–1," CBR.com, March 31, 2015. www.cbr.com.

28. John Martin, "'Saga' Artist Fiona Staples on Making Comics in a Digital Era," *New York Observer*, July 12, 2017. https://observer.com.

29. Quoted in Nathan Fox, "MoCCA Art Fest 2014 and Fiona Staples Q&A," Girls Gone Geek, March 15, 2014. https://girls-gone-geek.com.

30. Kelly Thompson, "Saga #2," CBR.com, April 16, 2012. www.cbr.com.

Chapter Three: Creating a Following

31. Quoted in Anthony Elio and Alex Moersen, "3 Comic Book Creators Share Their Original Stories," Innovation & Tech Today, September 28, 2018. https://innotechtoday.com.

32. Daniel Sharp, "Promoting Your Webcomic: Part 1—Free Options," *Demon Archives*, August 2015. https://demonarchives.com.

33. Quoted in Dom Carter, "Social Media for Artists: A Lifeline or a Curse?," Creative Bloq, August 9, 2018. www.creativebloq.com.

34. Quoted in Carter, "Social Media for Artists."

35. Quoted in Daniel Sharp, "Promoting Your Webcomic."

36. Quoted in Harron Walker, "*Snotgirl* Co-Creator Leslie Hung on Drawing Women and Embracing our 'Disgusting' Humanity," *Jezebel* (blog), September 27, 2018. https://jezebel.com.

37. Quoted in Mackenzie Pitcock, "Snot Everywhere: An Interview with *Snotgirl*'s Leslie Hung," *Women Write About Comics*, May 23, 2018. https://womenwriteaboutcomics.com.

38. Sharp, "Promoting Your Webcomic."

39. Derek Royal and Andy Kunka, "About the Show," Comics Alternative, 2018. http://comicsalternative.com.

40. Sharp, "Promoting Your Webcomic."

41. Quoted in Janelle Asselin, "Books That Feel Real: Spike Trotman on 'Poorcraft 2' and Building an Indie Comics Empire," Comics Alliance, December 12, 2014. https://web.archive

.org/web/20151208204133/http://comicsalliance.com/spike
-trotman-indie-comics-interview-poorcraft.

42. Caitlin Rosberg, "Self-Published Comics Are Changing an Aging Industry—for the Better," AV Club, June 20, 2016. www
.avclub.com.

43. Quoted in Steve Large, "*Beyond:* The Queer Sci-Fi & Fantasy Comic Anthology," Atlantic Books Today, April 29, 2016. http://atlanticbookstoday.ca.

44. Rosberg, "Self-Published Comics Are Changing an Aging Industry."

45. Quoted in Glen Weldon, "A Comics Convention for the Unconventional: The Small Press Expo," *All Things Considered*, NPR, September 20, 2016. www.npr.org.

46. Quoted in "Help with Promoting My Comic at Convention!," Tapas, August 3, 2018. https://forums.tapas.io.

Chapter Four: Graphic Novels Pushing Boundaries

47. Caitlin McCabe, "Will Eisner and the Mysterious Origin of the Graphic Novel," Comic Book Legal Defense Fund, December 23, 2015. http://cbldf.org.

48. Harvey, *The Art of the Comic Book*, p. 245.

49. Quoted in Michael Cavna, "Why 'Maus' Remains 'The Greatest Graphic Novel Ever Written,' 30 Years Later," *Washington Post*, August 11, 2016. www.washingtonpost.com.

50. Meryl Jaffe, "Using Graphic Novels in Education: *March: Book One*," Comic Book Legal Defense Fund, February 7, 2014. http://cbldf.org.

51. Quoted in A.J. Frost, "J. Krosoczka's Intimate Memoir *Hey Kiddo*," *The Beat* (blog), October 9, 2018. www.comicsbeat
.com.

52. Quoted in Kate Messner, "Writing About Addiction for Kids," *School Library Journal*, November 1, 2017. www.slj.com.

53. Quoted in Rowan Hisayo Buchanan, "An Intergalactic Tale Populated by Women," *Atlantic*, September 24, 2018. www
.theatlantic.com.

54. Buchanan, "An Intergalactic Tale Populated by Women."

55. Quoted in Sabaa Tahir, "Ms. Marvel: Why Does Marvel's Latest Book Succeed? Because Its New Muslim Teen Superhero Is 'Sweet, Conflicted and Immensely Relatable,'" *Entertainment* (blog), *Washington Post*, February 4, 2014. www.washingtonpost.com.

56. Aditi Shiva, "All in Your Hands Now: Review of *Ms. Marvel* Issue #2," *Aerogram*, April 9, 2014. http://theaerogram.com.

57. Quoted in Nicole Drum, "Ms. Marvel Kamala Khan Co-Creator Talks Diversity in Comics," ComicBook.com, December 30, 2017. https://comicbook.com.

FOR FURTHER RESEARCH

Informational Books

Comfort Love and Adam Withers, *The Complete Guide to Self-Publishing Comics*. New York: Watson-Guptill, 2015.

Hal Marcovitz, *Comic Book Art*. San Diego: ReferencePoint, 2016.

William Potter and Juan Calle, *The Ultimate Guide to Creating Comics*. London: Arcturus, 2017.

Barbara Slate, *You Can Do a Graphic Novel: Comic Books, Webcomics, and Strips*. Chicago: Britannica Digital Learning, 2018.

Fred Van Lente and Ryan Dunlavey, *Comic Book History of Comics: Birth of a Medium*. San Diego: IDW, 2017.

Graphic Novels

Will Eisner, *The Contract with God Trilogy: Life on Dropsie Avenue*. New York: W.W. Norton, 2005.

Jarrett J. Krosoczka, *Hey, Kiddo*. New York, Graphix, 2018.

John Lewis and Nate Powell, *March Trilogy*. Marietta, GA: Top Shelf, 2016.

Tilly Walden, *On a Sunbeam*. New York: First Second, 2018.

G. Willow Wilson and Adrian Alphona, *Ms. Marvel Volume 1: No Normal*. New York: Marvel, 2014.

Internet Sources

Rowan Hisayo Buchanan, "An Intergalactic Tale Populated by Women," *Atlantic*, September 24, 2018. www.theatlantic.com.

Anthony Elio and Alex Moersen, "3 Comic Book Creators Share Their Original Stories," Innovation & Tech Today, September 28, 2018. https://innotechtoday.com.

Mackenzie Pitcock, "Snot Everywhere: An Interview with *Snotgirl*'s Leslie Hung," *Women Write About Comics*, May 23, 2018. https://womenwriteaboutcomics.com.

Arlen Schumer, "Art & Comic Book Art," 13th Dimension, March 23, 2015. https://13thdimension.com.

Daniel Sharp, "Promoting Your Webcomic: Part 1—Free Options," *Demon Archives*, August 2015. https://demonarchives.com.

Websites

AV Club (www.avclub.com). One of the original entertainment websites, AV Club features an extensive library of reviews, interviews, and articles that cover comics, graphic novels, artists, creators, and comic books.

CBR.com (www.cbr.com). This website covers comics and comics-based current events, interviews, and reviews of movies, television shows, and videos. The comics community forum holds reader reviews and covers nearly every aspect of the comic book world.

Making Comics (www.makingcomics.com). The learning materials on this site are aimed at prospective comic book artists who want to find comprehensive information on writing, drawing, marketing, publishing, and selling comics. The site offers advice and links to art institutions and educational videos.

Webcomic Police (www.webcomicpolice.com). Creators of webcomics post their comics to this site, which allows readers to review and comment on the work. Visitors to the site can see the latest works in progress from their favorite artists, discover new artists, and offer their opinions on the comics.

Beat (www.comicsbeat.com). This blog covers comics, cartoonists, conventions, publishers, and video games in blogs, news articles, and reviews. Prospective comic artists can find a wealth of information about the industry on the "Resources: How to Break Into Comics and Survive Once You're There" section, which links to articles like "Advice for Aspiring Comic Artists Age 14–18" and "How to Launch a Self Published Comic."

Index

Note: Boldface page numbers indicate illustrations.

PICTURE CREDITS

Cover: Yogysic/iStockphoto.com

8: Marvel/Splash News/Newscom

13: Splash News/Newscom

17: Associated Press

23: Agencia el Universal/El Universal de Mexico/Newscom

29: Marvel Comics/Photofest

31: Nelvin C. Cepeda/San Diego Union/Newscom

34: Associated Press

41: Associated Press

50: Cartoon Network/Newscom

53: Associated Press

57: 2.4.7. Films/The Kennedy/Marshall Company/France 3 Cinema/Newscom

60: On a Sunbeam, First Second Books

ABOUT THE AUTHOR

Stuart A. Kallen is the author of more than 350 nonfiction books for children and young adults. He has written on topics ranging from the theory of relativity to the art of electronic dance music. In 2018 Kallen won a Green Earth book award from the Nature Generation environmental organization. In his spare time he is a singer, songwriter, and guitarist in San Diego.